Facts, Folklore and Feasts of Christmas

Beatrice Holloway

TSL Publications

First published in Great Britain in 2019
By TSL Publications, Rickmansworth

Copyright © 2019 Beatrice Holloway
Cover: https://pixabay.com/photos/christmas-christmas-tree-decorate-1869902/

ISBN / 978-1-913294-24-3

DEDICATION

Denis John
30.10.1927 – 29.12.2012

About Beatrice

Beatrice has written a number of children's books: *Towing Path Tales*, *More Towing Path Tales* and *A Particular Year* as well as a number of science experiments for children – all available as ebooks.

The London Borough of Hillingdon library service has published two of her children's stories and awarded her with a Certificate of merit – 'In recognition of an outstanding contribution to the Arts'. Beatrice was also awarded a Lottery Grant to write a commissioned historical play: *Commoner to Coronet*.

Three adult books, *A Man from the North East*, *Elusive Destiny* and *Archie's Children* were published recently. Beatrice is a retired teacher and a member of The Society of Women Writers and Journalists and the Society of Authors. She has been a member of a local writing group – Phrase Writers – for over twelve years and is the children's storyteller for Hillingdon Narrowboats Association.

Prologue

There is so much writing and research about Christmas that I hesitated to begin this book. Truth to tell curiosity, in the end, compelled me to begin. What a journey it has proved to be, so much information.

In the Christian world, it is a little disconcerting to learn that the foundations of some of our favourite rituals are based on pagan traditions. Pagan, in this work, embraces all aspects of religion, customs and ceremonies of pagan time, some of which included human sacrifices to their gods. How clever of the early church dignitaries to embrace and soften these long-held pagan rites.

Many questions have been raised about the timing of Christ's birth. The telling of his birth to the trusting, illiterate populace of the past, was magical, a birthday to celebrate.

What, then, is the truth or what is fiction? Much has been left out. To be honest, I have selected information that intrigued me or I just didn't know. The fact remains, that the combination of the celebrations, should it be the winter solstice or the birth of Christ, is a joyful time, a time to give, not only of presents, but a time to give goodwill to our loved ones and strangers.

I have chosen to share with you, some of my interesting discoveries, as well as a few Christmas experiences of my family and friends. I do hope that you enjoy your reading.

Earlier Times

Christmas! Just saying the word evokes all sorts of emotions. Always there are the children's anticipation and annual questions: 'Who is St Nicholas, Father Christmas or Santa Claus?' to start with. They begin to wonder what present they might get. Is it the one they asked or hoped for? From mid-October, they, and many adults, start to think of Christmas, and begin counting the days.

Everyone begins to wonder what presents to buy for whom. Will s/he like this? Am I spending too much? Is the size/colour right? Who should they invite to share the day? Your parents, mine, other family members or maybe a lonely neighbour? Then there is deciding what dish to serve for the festive meal. Should it be beef this year, or fish perhaps? Nearly always, in the end, it is a turkey in pride of place on the table. Endless dilemmas.

There are many debates worldwide as to the actual birth date of Jesus. The Bible does not give any date. What we do know is that shepherds were not in the fields during December. December, in Judea, is cold and rainy, and it is likely the shepherds would have sought shelter for their flocks at night. Therefore, the birthday might well be during summer or early autumn. We also know that censuses were not held in the winter months when temperatures were often below freezing and the roads in poor condition, making a journey hazardous for anyone who was pregnant. So, maybe not a birthday, rather a celebration of the birth of Jesus.

Not only is the time of the birth suspect, so too is the appearance of the star at that time.

King James Bible, Matthew 2.2, states that when the Magi, who had arrived from the East, were questioned by Herod, they replied, 'We saw His star in the east and have come to worship him.' It is accepted in Christian churches that there were three wise men, as only three gifts were recorded. Who were the Magi? Was their true identity lost in translation? Were they wise men, kings, magicians or astrologers? A thesaurus gives Magi an alternative meaning, 'Zoroastrian priests in ancient Media and Persia, reputed to possess supernatural powers.' Astrologers were deemed evil by the early church. Therefore, it is likely that they thought 'wise men' a suitable alternative.

The Orient suggests that there were twelve men, but a painting in the cemetery of Saints Peter and Marcellinus show only two. In the Kircher Museum, Los Angeles, eight are depicted on a vase. The cemetery of Domitilla shows four. The accepted Magi were, Melchior, Caspar and Balthazar and were said to have come from Arabia, Persia and India. They would have travelled 900 miles west to reach Bethlehem. Therefore, they could not have seen a star in the east to follow.

It has been suggested that the Magi might have followed a bright meteor, comet or supernova. However, meteors although bright, flash and are gone when reaching the earth's atmosphere, so nothing lasting to follow.

Possibly a comet, but the nearest sighting of a comet (Halley's Comet) was 11 BC – sometime before the birth of

Jesus. At that time, comets were believed to be bad omens. Nor, it is believed, was there a supernova. If seen, it could be seen for a few weeks only. The only one noted at the time was in the wrong direction in the sky for the Magi to follow.

Another possibility is a planet. In those far off days, planets would have been defined as 'wandering stars'. It is possible that there was a planetary conjunction, when planets appear close to one another. This would be visible for a few days or longer, depending on the planets involved. Astronomers have calculated that for ten months in 7 BC Jupiter and Saturn were very close to each other. In February 6 BC, Mars joined them.

In the New English Bible, the Magi's reply to Herod, was, 'We observed the rising of His star and have come to pay Him homage.' Recent research suggests that the debate of the identity of the Magi and star goes on.

Despite these theories, and there are more, the Star of Bethlehem remains a firm favourite within the story of Christmas.

How then was 25 December chosen? Nearly all the Christmas traditions we are familiar with are rooted in the Pagan celebrations. The word 'pagan' is loosely thought to mean cults of obscure religions that believed in a variety of gods. The Druids throughout Europe were one such group. The origin of the word 'Druid' is not certain and it is possible that it comes from 'doire', a Gaelic word for oak tree. The oak was considered to have knowledge and wisdom. The natural world and its powers were the main concern of the Druids, in particular trees, especially the oak. Wood was a precious commodity, as it provided shelter, fuel, ships, weapons and some provided food. The author, Robert Macfarlane, tells us that the Welsh saying, 'dod yn atfy nghoed' literally means, 'to return to my trees'.

One of the most important Druid celebrations was the Yule or Saturnalia time. These customs were, in turn, embraced by the early church and continued to please all who were converted to Christianity later. The date of Yule in the northern hemisphere falls between December 20 to December 23, depending on the year in the Gregorian calendar. No matter what religion, cult or community, it was a joyous time for the population. It was the time of rebirth of the sun after the longest dark night of the year. It was regarded as a sign of rebirth of nature's fertility – ensuring new life and harvests for another year.

One tradition at that time was the ceremony involving the yule log. Each year a log, preferably from an ash tree, was collected from the woods and placed in a hearth. Next, it was doused with either cider or ale, decorated with greenery and then set on fire, if possible, with a taper from last year's log. The log should be big enough to smoulder for twelve days before being extinguished.

Besides Sun gods, the ceremony was also thanks to a number of other deities. The best known are Dragda and Brighid the daughter of Dragda. Brighid is believed to be the Goddess of doctors, poets, smiths, fire and hearth, childbirth and of warfare, and her soldiers were known as brigands.

The greenery decorations referred to included holly, ivy, rosemary and mistletoe, each supposedly having mystical powers. In pagan times, holly was considered to be a male plant. The early Christian church incorporated it into the celebrations by suggesting that the white flowers symbolized Christ's purity; the bitter bark, his suffering on the cross and the prickly leaves formed the crown of thorns at the crucifixion. Lastly, the red berries represented his blood where he was pricked with the thorns.

Ivy, like holly, is an evergreen plant and represented eternal affection or love due to its clinging nature. It is able to grow in almost any environment. It is a perennial and thus represented immortality.

Have you ever been kissed under mistletoe? The Druids thought it possessed powers to bring good luck and dispel evil spirits. It was also used to poison human sacrifices. The idea of kissing under the mistletoe was included in Christmas festivals by Christians, a token to the druids' sexual rituals during Saturnalia.

It was also a sign of love and friendship. Mistletoe is a parasite, its seeds are deposited in a host tree by bird droppings. However, associating mistletoe with romance is entirely spoilt when one learns that the word mistletoe is derived from two Anglo Saxon words; mistle meaning dung and tan meaning twig or stick – that is to say bird droppings on a stick!

Rosemary symbolises remembrance and honouring the dead. Its Latin name was *Ros Maris*, translated 'dew of the sea', as its original habitat was on the seashore. Now, the Latin name is *Rosmarinus officinalis*.

Sir Tomas More (1478-1535), refers to it as Rosmarine, and wrote, 'I lett it runne all over my garden walls, not onlie because my bees love it, but because it is the herb sacred to remembrance, and, therefore, to friendship; whence a sprig of it hath a dumb language that maketh it the chosen emblem of our funeral wakes and in our burial grounds.'

Shakespeare refers to the plant in Ophelia's speech in Hamlet: 'There's rosemary, that's for remembrance. Pray you, love, remember.' In Romeo and Juliet, Juliet asks her nurse, 'Doth not Rosemary and Romeo begin with a letter?' and Friar Laurence at Juliet's burial, says, 'Dry up your tears, and stick your rosemary on this fair corse,' (corpse). Rosemary also appears in *A Winter's Tale*, 'For you there's rosemary and rue ...'

Greek scholars wore wreaths of rosemary to aid their memories when taking exams. Brides would place the herb in their bouquet, headpiece, and dress. Wedding guests were given sprigs to wear to remind them of the special occasion. Rosemary was sometimes added to the couple's wine to remind them of their solemn vows. There was an old saying 'where rosemary flourished, the woman ruled.' Needless to say, the plant was soon uprooted by husbands!

Rosemary has many medicinal benefits. At one time it was used as a cure for indigestion, headaches and joint and muscle aches. One of the earliest printed references to the herb is in Rycharde Banckes' book *Banckes' Herbal* printed in 1525, which stated that, '... boyle them in fayre water and drinke that water for it is much worthe against all manner of evils in the body.'

As a symbol of remembrance and fidelity, sprigs are worn by Australians and New Zealanders on Anzac day. It is a common plant growing wild on the Gallipoli peninsula and is often used as a hedging plant around their war memorials.

This herb is also sacred to Mary because it is believed that the aroma was first noticed when baby Jesus' swaddling clothes were hung on a rosemary bush to dry.

Wreaths in ancient Egypt, Rome, Greece and Persia were symbolic of status, authority, and warrior prowess. Wreaths were also awarded to winning athletes and poets. It was during the sixteenth century that wreaths were brought into homes in Europe. According to Ace Collins, when the Christmas tree was trimmed to shape (see next chapter), the trimmings were woven into a wreath. This was in a time when nothing was wasted. At first, they were used to decorate the tree, but because of its perfect shape, a circle that has no end, to Christians it represented eternity. The Advent wreath might hold three purple and one pink candle. Lighting the first purple candle was for hope. The second Sunday of Advent the candle is known as the Bethlehem candle, and when lit, represents love and Jesus' manager. The third candle called the shepherd candle, lit on the third Sunday represents joy. The last candle known as Angel's Candle is for peace. Today, some wreaths also have a white candle to represent the pure life of Christ, white being the colour of purity.

The Christmas Tree

We can trace the custom of worshipping and dressing of trees back to the pagan traditions of many cults. There were mythical beliefs of a sacred tree, and the Old Testament in the Bible tells of the Tree of Life and The Tree of Knowledge of Good and Evil in the Garden of Eden (Genesis 2:8b-9). Also in the Bible, is the condemnation of worshippers of trees (Jeremiah 10, King James Version). We must not forget that in the past, wood was a precious commodity in many parts of the world. It is not surprising, therefore, that trees were worshipped, in particular the yew and oak.

Druids used a wand made from yew to ward off evil spirits. They believed wells had healing powers if situated near growing yews. These trees were also symbolic of longevity and fertility. The yew wood, being one of the strongest and pliant, was favoured in the making of longbows.

At the time of the Winter Solstice, people would decorate trees and, again, the Christian church embraced this custom to win Pagans into the Christian faith. Among the many legends of how the fir tree became the symbol of Christianity is one attributed to an eighth-century English monk Boniface, a missionary in Germany. It seemed that one day he saw some people making sacrifices before an ancient oak to their sacred God, Thor. So enraged was Boniface that he took an axe and felled the tree in order to end the worship of a false idol. The pagan folk were convinced he would be struck down by lightning. As nothing untoward happened to Boniface, he used the event to convert them to Christianity. When a fir sapling grew from the fallen oak, the church decreed that the fir became a symbol of Christ. It was thought that as it was triangular in shape it represented the trinity, the Father, Son and Holy Spirit — and from there came the idea that the tree should be a symbol of Christ and new life. By bringing a tree into our homes and decorating it, we are following yet another ancient custom.

Research by Alison Barnes suggests who really introduced the modern way of dressing trees at Christmas. Although this may or may not be so, it is said that Martin Luther, a friend of Queen Charlotte, was walking through a forest near his home one winter's evening. He looked up and saw thousands of stars glittering like jewels among the branches of trees. So enchanted with the scene, he decorated a tree in his home with lit candles for his children. By 1605 fir, box or yew trees in Germany were being decorated in many dwellings.

The decorating of a Christmas yew branch was first introduced in England when Charlotte came from Germany to marry King George III. The yew boughs adorned with gifts and lighted tapers greatly impressed all at court. Later yew trees were potted and decorated at Christmastime. In a short time, the idea of decorated Christmas trees for the more well-off upper-classes was quickly adopted, especially at children's parties.

Although Prince Albert, Queen Victoria's consort, is credited with introducing the lovely idea of household decorated fir trees, it was the descriptive publication in magazines of the royal fir trees during the mid-1840/50s that the custom of a Christmas tree, in almost every home, became the norm.

One the most popular decorations hanging on Christmas trees is the glass bauble. Their origin can be traced back to the sixteenth century. It was in the town of Lauscha, Germany and the glass blowing skills of its inhabitants, who first produced Christmas ornaments. In the nineteenth century, the factory began producing fruit and nut shaped glass ornaments. These were decorated with mercury or lead to give a silvery finish. As their ornaments grew in popularity, other glassworks began to produce their own style of decorations, including animals, saints, angels and children. FW Woolworth, on a visit to Germany, realised their commercial value and began to import the ornaments, firstly to the United States and then to his worldwide stores.

Who has not, as a child, handmade decorations for the tree and home? One favourite in my childhood was buying sticky strips of coloured paper to make a chain. With my

siblings we were able to festoon the living room. With the help of brass drawing pins, the chains were pinned to the wooden picture rail. The picture shows decorations made with a craft group one Christmas.

One last interesting note is that the lack of a tree in the White House in 1902 was due to the fact that President Theodore Roosevelt had not ordered one by 23 December.

The time of giving

Presents were handed out in the New Year long before Rome accepted Christianity. The ruling Emperors, during Saturnalia celebrations, commanded the poor and lower class citizens to bring offerings and presents. Later, present giving became normal practice for the rich and poor. The presents given at that time were defined by social status. The poem 'Sportula' in *Present Giving* by Martial, a poet, 40 AD, lists some of the gifts. Writing tablets, dice, money boxes, combs, perfumes, toothpicks, parrots, a slave and rare animals, to name a few.

The giving of presents at Christmastime was another adoption from paganism. Early in 300 AD, it was decreed by the church, that Christ's, supposedly birth date, should be celebrated every 25 December. The church later suggested that the giving of gifts was related to the Three Wise Men, the Magi, who gave gifts to the infant Jesus.

Following the Roman Emperor's maxim, Queen Elizabeth I, set out a tariff that dictated who should give her what. It is recorded that one Archbishop had to tender £40, equivalent to approximately £9,500 in today's currency. Amongst the personal presents she received, was a satin nightgown from Sir Francis Walsingham.

In Queen Victoria's time, presents for her children included swords and other military weapons. Prince Albert was given a portrait of his wife as a seven year old and a book of Lord Tennyson's poems.

Although the time to give presents varies from country to country and family to family, it was during the 1800s that present giving was finally established on 25 December. The Victorians, on December 26th gave out Christmas Boxes and time off to their servants. The 26th is also Saint Stephen's Day and it was a tradition of churches to collect donations in a box for the poor. Scholars have put forward other suggestions of this tradition. One custom was that tradesmen, on the first working day after Christmas Day, would collect their 'boxes' of money or gifts in acknowledgement of their good service over the year. Yet another suggestion put forward relates to a custom of sailing ships taking aboard a box containing money. This custom was thought to bring good luck to the sailors. The box would be given to a priest who opened it on Boxing Day and distributed its contents to the poor.

Pagans believed one of their Gods, Woden with a long flowing white beard, travelled through the skies in winter. This is thought to be the origins of Father Christmas. In order to convert the followers of Woden, the Catholic Church matched these celebrations to that of Saint Nicholas, held on the date of his death, 6th December. He was accused of blasphemy and was stoned to death.

Saint Nicholas was born in 270 AD of wealthy parents and orphaned in his early teens. He had a reputation of generosity and the story of three, betrothed sisters, without a dowry who then found their stockings, hanging over the fire to dry, filled with gold is attributed to Nicholas. Thus the tradition of hanging up a stocking on Christmas Eve stems from the tale.

Saint Nicholas, was a bearded bishop and portrayed in canon robes of red, perhaps the forerunner of the more familiar plump, white bearded man in red clothing, and known as Father Christmas to children. In 1809, Washington Irving, an American Victorian author, refers to Father Christmas by his Dutch name, *Sinterklass*, Santa Claus. In 1822, Dr Clements wrote the classic poem based on Father Christmas, 'The night before Christmas' but referred to him as Saint Nicholas. In the poem he tells of Saint Nicholas travelling with sleigh and reindeers. This could be interpreted as a nod to Woden's sky travelling. Entering homes via the chimney, might be a slight acknowledgement of Saint Nicholas finding empty stockings in the fire place.

It was Thomas Nast, a Bavarian illustrator, who almost completed the Santa Claus we are familiar with today. From 1862 through 1886, based on Moore's poem, Nast drew cartoon images of Santa for *Harper's Weekly*. Earlier pictures of Saint Nicholas showed him as a stern looking bishop, Nash portrayed him as a gnome-like figure in a green frock.

In 1931, the Swedish commercial artist Haddon Sundblom was contracted by the Coca Cola Corporation to create a coke-drinking Santa. Santa was modelled by Sundblom on his friend Lou Prentice, a cheerful, man with a chubby face. However, as stated earlier, Saint Nicholas, the bishop, had a long flowing, white beard and was dressed in a red ceremonial gown. The corporation insisted that Santa's suit be bright Coca Cola red. Either deliberately, or not, Father Christmas, Santa Claus or Saint Nicholas are now always dressed in red, perhaps another reminder of the past.

Yet another saint may have influenced the present giving traditions. Good King Wenceslas, also referred to as Saint Wenceslas, 107-929, was raised a Christian by his paternal grandmother, Saint Ludmila. She was murdered by Wenceslas's mother, Dragomir, a pagan. When Wenceslas, a duke, not a king, came of age he became head of the government. He was determined the conflicts between Christian and non-Christian factions in Bohemia should end. His plans to spread the Christian faith, however, antagonized his pagan opponents. After submitting to German King Henry 1, Wenceslas' brother, Boleslaus was encouraged, by the nobles of the court who had disapproved of the surrender, to murder him. It is believed that as Wenceslas was on his way to mass, he was killed at the church door.

Wenceslas introduced an education system allowing commoners to read and write. He improved the laws and formed a more fair-minded government. He was greatly respected for good deeds towards the poor and needy and his Christian faith.

A text by the Bohemian Chronicler, Cosmas of Prague 1119 states, 'His deeds I think you know better than I could tell you; for, as is read in his Passion, no one doubts that, rising every night from his noble bed, with bare feet and only one chamberlain, he went around to God's churches and gave alms generously to widows, orphans, those in prison and afflicted by every difficulty.'

John M Neale (1818-1866) based the lyrics of 'Good King Wenceslas' on the life of King Wenceslas, written circa 1850 to celebrate Saint Stephen's Day. At that time, it was not well received having no reference at all to Christ's birthday.

Who then is Kris Kringle? In the sixteenth century, these saints were not so popular in Europe. Who, then became the giver of presents? In the UK, it was 'Father Christmas', someone in children's stories of old. In France, it was 'Père Nöel'. In Germany, the bringer of gifts was the Christ Child or 'Christ Kind', called 'Kris Kringle' by early US settlers. Later, the settlers reverted to the old stories of Saint Nicholas, and Kris Kringle became 'Sinterklass' or as we now say 'Santa Claus'. It is also believed that Kris Kringle is, in fact, Secret Santa.

Another bringer of Christmas gifts especially to the Dutch communities in Pennsylvania is *Belsh-nichel*. The meaning of his name can mean either 'Nicholas in Fur' or 'Flog Nicholas'. He is very frightening and severe. He carries a switch to be struck across the back of naughty children. For better behaved children there are sweets.

Pets are still given as presents, not wild ones, but sometimes exotic. However, some of the presents given today are equally as bizarre as giving a slave. Selected from the magazine, *Good Housekeeping* website 2015, are some of the 'Worst Christmas Gifts' received. Supplied anonymously, they included, a six year old given a shoe polishing kit, a Balinese death mask from a boyfriend, a clothes de-bobbler from a grandma for a thirteen year old and someone else received eight tins of tomato soup from their father. Another website, *Offbeat*, listed among the twenty-five worst presents ever, was, 'a bottle of Miracle Grow, at age thirteen, from my mom. "For your boobs," she said'.

Friends and acquaintances told me of their strange presents. One has family in Australia. Every Christmas a large parcel was sent, packed with gifts with an Australian theme. Her children were always excited when it arrived, usually well in advance of the big day. Image then, the children bursting with anticipation. The presents, properly labelled were handed out after dinner. A sunhat with cork bobbles for one caused much laughter, a tee shirt with the Australian map printed across the chest for another. But what a shock for the youngest child. Carefully, he unwrapped his present. Firstly, there was the look of incredulity on his face, followed by a look of disappointment and tears. The present? A kangaroo skin, and sellotaped to it, a note explaining the hole in the skin was a bullet hole.

Another family witnessed the distress of a ten years old. Every year without fail, his favourite uncle would be late for dinner, but always with a great present. This particular year, on opening the present the child was so disappointed. Instead of, perhaps, a toy steam roller or a meccano set, he received a white, nylon school shirt. One elderly person received a damp blouse that had been purchased in a charity shop, washed and packed in haste.

Entering into the spirit of the annual Secret Santa idea, I once received a tin of biscuits. Always welcome and useful, but these were two years out of date.

We, should, of course, be grateful for all we receive, even those from thoughtless people or confused elderly relatives, but the truth be known, getting naff presents makes a funny story to tell in later years.

To end this chapter, in case you didn't know, the grand total of Christmas gifts in the popular Christmas song, 'The Twelve Days of Christmas', adds up to three hundred and sixty-four!

A History of Carols

Songs were sung at the winter solstice in past times. The Greek poet Lucian wrote that drunken people called at houses naked, singing (wassailing) and rapping whilst eating biscuits shaped in the human form.

Wassail was an alcoholic beverage of mulled mead or cider, flavoured with apples in a communal bowl, and drunk liberally by all on the last day of the winter solstice celebrations. A fire was lit in an orchard and dancing and singing incantations were made to the apple trees, in the hope of encouraging a bountiful harvest. This tradition, to a certain extent, changed and wassailing became the toast for someone's good health. When Saint Boniface visited Rome in 742 he observed and complained that during the Christmas days, people were 'singing and dancing in the streets in pagan style'.

By the Middle Ages, wassailing or carol singing, became a forced hand of present giving, and had become a practice of, as Lucas Reilly states, 'boozy begging'. The poor would approach their richer neighbours and sip from the wassailing bowl, or fill their own bowl. They would then perform songs, wishing him good health and wealth. In medieval times, singing and dancing, the word carol once meant dance, was held in the churches, following the pagan tradition. It was deemed that the caroling interfered with the holy masses of Christmas. In order to keep the mass sacred, the dignitaries sent the carol singers outside.

Early musicians gave followers solemn Christian songs. One such song was called 'Angels' Hymn'. Another choral hymn was *Festa Christi* c. 900 AD by Notker Balbulus and complaints were made that long verses 'taxed one's memory'. During the 1000s, hymns celebrating Christmas contained a surfeit of Alleluias. European composers began writing Christmas carols, that later became known as songs of praise. As they were in Latin they did not prove to be very popular.

However, by the seventeenth century, it is recorded that groups of drunken, noisy men and boys were playing music, shooting off their guns and, sometimes destroying property. Little wonder that the Puritans in the 1640s banned Christmas carols, but it seems the carols survived as people sang them in secret.

The revival of singing in church began in Victorian times and choirs were formed. There was a demand for Christmas songs and many carols were written in that era and are now familiar to us. It is surprising to learn that a number of them were adopted from earlier times. The cheerful, 'Deck the Halls' dates back to the sixteenth century, a Welsh melody, and was published in 1862 when the English lyrics were written by Thomas Oliphant.

In Charles Dickens's book, *A Christmas Carol* published in 1843, he wrote, '... at the first sound of "God Bless you Merry gentlemen" ... Scrooge seized the ruler with such energy of action that the singer fled in terror ...' The lyrics were published in 1833 anonymously, but it is believed it was sung in churches in the fifteenth century, and may have been sung by roving bands of singers in taverns.

It was Charles Wesley who wrote the words of 'Hark how all the Welkin Ring' in 1739. Welkin was an old term for the heavens. Today's version, 'Hark the Herald Angels Sing' was published in 1753 by George Whitefield, who changed the first line. The words were sung to various tunes, but in 1856 William Cummings joined the lyrics to one of Felix Mendelssohn's score. This was written in 1840 to celebrate a German festival celebrating the introduction of printing. At that time Mendelssohn believed it would be welcomed by singers, and said, 'but it will never do to sacred words'.

The Christmas carol 'Christians awake! Salute the happy morn', was written in 1745 by John Byrom. It was a gift for his favourite daughter, Dorothy, and was first known as 'Christmas Day for Dolly'. Byrom studied at Trinity College, Cambridge and studied medicine in France. However, in 1716 he didn't think he had enough qualifications to set up a practice. Instead, he taught his system of shorthand known as New Universal Shorthand. By circa 1740 this was being used by the clerk in the House of Lords and the brothers, John and Charles Wesley. Byrom was also a poet and coined the phrase Tweedledum and Tweedledee, a satirical witticism of the dispute about the styles and merits of Handel and Bononcini music.

'Dulci Jubilo', it is believed by scholars, was written in 1328 by Heinrich Seuse in a mixture of Medieval German and Latin. An early tune dates back to c. 1400 although it is possible the tune was known in Europe earlier. During the sixteen hundreds, another verse was added, thought to have been written by Martin Luther. In 1853, John Mason Neale translated the carol and titled the work 'Good Christian Men, Rejoice' and in Arthur T Russell's translation he suggested the work was, 'Now Sing We, Now Rejoice'. This carol was the second most popular carol, the *BBC Music Magazine* survey (2008) reveals.

While researching the history of my chosen carols, I accepted that the words and music were always written by men. It has been difficult to find carols by women. 'Once in Royal David's City' was written by Cecil F Alexander. The name Cecil is familiar to me as my father had a friend of that name. As I continued looking, mostly on the Internet, for more information on Cecil, Mrs Cecil Frances Alexander came up on the screen. I was surprised and delighted that I had, at last found a woman, a very talented one, who had written a Christmas carol.

The carol, 'Once in Royal David's City' began as a poem by Mrs Alexander. It was published in 1848 in a hymn book entitled, *Hymns for Little Children*. It proved very popular and there were at least sixty-nine editions. It was intended as an explanation to questions that children often asked. One such question, 'Where was Jesus born?' and the poem was written as the answer. The poem was discovered by Henry John Gauntlett, an organist who set it to music a year later. The proceeds of her book funded the Londonderry and Raphoe Diocesan Institution for the education of the Deaf and Dumb, which was founded in Strabane. Her other charitable work included the Derry Home for Fallen Women, and she developed a district nursing service.

Mrs Alexander was the wife of the Bishop of London-derry and wrote many religious poems for children. Her works include, 'There is a Green Hill far Away' that answered the question of, 'Why did He have to die?' To the question, 'Who made the World?', the reply was, 'All things bright and Beautiful'.

Another Victorian female to write a carol was Christina Rossetti. Christina was invited to write a Christmas poem for the American magazine *Scribner's Monthly*. Her poem was originally called, 'A Christmas Carol', known now as 'In the Bleak Midwinter' and was printed in 1872.

Gusav Holst was asked to compose music for different hymns that were to be published in book form. He chose to compose his music about somewhere that had influenced his life. For 'In the Bleak Midwinter', he chose Cranham, a place where his grandparents lived. Boyhood visits of Christmas in Cranham woods with holly and ivy in abundance reinforced his Christmas memories. Rossetti's poem was finally set to his music in 1906, twelve years after her death from cancer.

Other work by Rossetti was influenced by two factors. She was deeply religious and a volunteer at the Saint Mary Magdalene prison in Highgate. Here she had contact with prostitutes and unmarried mothers, prompting her to write about illegitimacy, illicit love and the role of women in the nineteenth century. Rossetti's wide range of prose and poetry relate to friendship and mortality.

Her work also includes nursery rhymes for children. *Sing-Song: A Nursery Rhyme Book (1872)* and a fairy tale book: *Speaking Likenesses* (1874).

These poems, later to become carols, were written when women had neither the vote nor property rights. But, because of their work, they were accepted into a male dominated world where women had little status. Sarah Gillespie wrote, 'subversively perhaps, they ensured that a female agenda was sung out ... by men and women alike.'

Throughout time, the words of carols have been subtlety altered by children and adults. The rhyming and rhythm are maintained, so that the singer hopes there is no chance of being found out. Who has not sung, 'While Shepherds wash their socks by night?' I certainly did. In 'Hark the Herald Angels sing', the second line was sung as 'Beecham's pills are just the thing!' However, extremely popular in 1938 this carol gained new words, 'Hark the Herald angels sing, Mrs Simpson's pinched our king!' A sentiment held by many at the time.

Sometimes words are altered by children who, perhaps, did not understand the words or mishear. A few examples collected from *Creative Youth Ideas* on the Internet, include:

'We three kings of porridge and tar', 'Noel, Noel, Barney's the king of Israel' and 'Come and froggy faithful.'

Carols are an important compliment to the Christmas festivities, but equally enjoyed are the seasonal, often humorous, traditional songs. 'Chestnuts roasting on an Open Fire' was first titled was, 'The Christmas Song'. It was written in 1945 during an oppressively hot summer. Bob Wells had jotted down the first four lines. When questioned by his co-writer, Mel Torme, Wells, according to Mel's son, said, 'I thought that maybe if I could just write down a few lines of wintry verse, I could physiologically get an edge over this heat.' Within in the hour, 'The Christmas Song' was completed. Although written by Mel Torme, a crooner, it was Nat King Cole who recorded the song in 1946. A parody of the song was written by Mick Terry. It is said that after he left the fire screen open, twice, sparks flew out and the sitting room carpet was set on fire. These occurrences prompted him to write,

Chestnuts Roasting on an open Fire
But open flames tend to shoot so much higher,
And sparks jump out where they're exposed.

'Let it Snow, Let it Snow, let it Snow' is another Christmas song written during the 1946 heat wave. It is interesting to note that Christmas is not mentioned in the lyrics. The theme centres on time spent in front of a cosy fire with loved ones. It seems that on the hottest day of the year, Sammy Cahn suggested to Jule Stein, that they cool off at the beach. Stein replied, 'Let's stay in and write a winter song.' Together the penned the words and music.

There is much speculation as to what time of year the most successful song ever, 'White Christmas', was written by Irving Berlin. The first verse, rarely heard nowadays, begins,

The sun is shining,
the grass is green,
The orange and palm trees sway.
There's never been such a day,
In Beverly Hills, LA
But it's December the 24th,
And I am longing to be up north ...

It was written as a satire to be sung in a musical revue, *Holiday Inn* where people were having a drink beside a swimming pool, shaded by palm trees. Paramount Studios began filming in 1941. Bing Crosby first sang this song, including the first verse, 24 December 1941, on the radio. In that same December, America declared war on Japan after the Pearl Harbour attack. The lyrics touched the hearts of enlisted Americans going overseas, particularly the line, 'just like the ones I used to know'. Berlin acknowledged the sentiments of the uniformed personnel, and instructed his publisher that in future sheet music, the first verse should be omitted.

Readers might be interested to know that work on this manuscript was being typed, during the record breaking summer of 2019 when 101c was recorded in Cambridgeshire.

There are many Christmas/winter songs to choose from, and 'The Twelve Days of Christmas' was once considered a carol, and believed to date from 1714. William Henry Husk, a historian of music in the nineteenth century, 1864, stated that the carol was found on a broadside, printed in Newcastle upon Tyne, that showed the song was sung at various periods during the last hundred and fifty years. The words were printed in a children's book, *Mirth without Mischief*, 1780. It was a memory game to be played on the Twelfth Night. People taking part were required to memorise and repeat what others had added to a round-robin story. The gifts were varied in different versions of the game and some were tongue-twisters. Defaulters had to pay a forfeit, usually a kiss or a sweet.

However, there is a school of thought that originally the song was a secret code for Catholics. From Queen Elizabeth I's time, Mass was forbidden and punishable. Practicing priests could be banished or charged with treason for which they could be hung, drawn and quartered. People following the Catholic faith or protecting a priest could not vote, hold property, have weapons or be a witness in court cases. In April 1829, George IV signed the Emancipation Bill, granting freedom of worship.

There are a number of History Myth Debunkers on the Internet, from which I gleaned the following. It appears that the song originated in France, a Catholic country (persecuting Protestants) and had no need to have songs with secret religious meanings. *Mirth without Mischief*'s title page states, 'Sung at King Pepin's ball.' There is no English King Pepin, but Pepin III, known as Pepin the Short, was the father of Charlemagne. Pepin ruled from 752 to 768. The Debunkers also added that the partridge was only introduced into East Anglia around 1770 from France.

Another theory for this traditional song's words, suggests that it is a love song. Professor of classics Edward Phinney, University of Massachusetts in an interview said, 'you realise they're all gifts from a lover to a woman.' He suggested that the partridge in a pear tree for example might be a fertility symbol. The pear represented the heart and the partridge, along with the other birds mentioned, was considered to be an aphrodisiac. The eight maids a milking and nine ladies dancing, along with the pipers and drummers could be wedding guests. 'The whole song',

Phinney concluded, 'seems to me to point to a festival of joy and love more appropriate to a secular holiday.'

Some people, particularly towards the end of the song, find it becomes boring. However, it has a cheerful tune and the words may well be altered again and again in the coming years, but it is a timeless favourite song.

The Christmas Cracker

What would your Christmas dinner table or party be without crackers or, as they were first called, cosaques? First, there is the bang, sometimes unexpected when pulled between two people. They shake their half to see if they have the gift hidden inside. Next is the placing of the ridiculous paper hat nearly always perched askew, then the reading of the jokes that bring out heartfelt groans when the answers are revealed. During the festive season a number of newspapers and magazines, *The Independent*, *The Mirror*, *Daily Mail*, *Metro*, *Yours* magazine and various radio stations list the worst jokes found in crackers.

Why did the pony have to gargle?
Because it was a little horse.

It was Tom Smith, a London confectioner, who first produced crackers in England. It was after a visit to Paris in 1840 where he was intrigued to see bon bon's, sugared almonds, twisted in colourful paper. On his return to London, he decided to copy the idea. At first they were not popular even though he included a small love motto or riddle.

It is said that one evening when sitting in front of his fire, the burning logs gave out sparks and made a crack sound. He thought it might be fun to open his crackers with a similar sound. It was two years before he could find a way to make such a crack. The answer lay in silver fulminate. The chemical was discovered earlier in the century by an English chemist, Edward C Howard. Further development of the chemical was made later by professor, Luigi Valentino Brugnatelli, an Italian chemist. It is an explosive and sensitive to impact and heat. At one time it was used as a detonator in UK firearms. The crack sound is created by sandpaper coated in the chemical, and when the cracker is pulled, friction, therefore heat, is caused between the papers and ... BANG! In order for the idea to work, the twist of paper was not suitable and needed enlarging to accommodate the impregnated strip. A cardboard tube was the answer. Once pulled, who can forget the distinctive gunpowder smell?

What do you give a dog for Christmas?
A mobile bone.

Tom Smith's three sons inherited the growing business and now it is the cracker we know today. Once the cracker is pulled, nearly always the first item the recipient searches for is the gift. Depending on the size and quality of the cracker these range from plastic moustaches, false teeth, corkscrews, nail clippers and many more. Millionaires' crackers that may well cost over £200 each, contain items of gold, silver pens, cuff links or jewellery.

What do snowmen have for breakfast?

Snowflakes.

The brothers created themed crackers. These included ones for bachelors and spinsters, Charlie Chaplin, the Scout movement and in the 1930s the channel tunnel, and the Suffragettes. Alice Maude Mary Arncliffe Sennett (1862-1936) was an actress and a strong Suffragette supporter. With her husband she carried on the trade of her father, an Italian confectioner, manufacturing ornamental confectionery and crackers. In 1914, they produced Votes for Women crackers in the suffragettes movement's colours of violet, white and green. These were made a year after Emily Davison died under the king's horse at the Derby on 8 June 1913.

What does Father Christmas do when his elves misbehave?

He gives them the sack.

Crackers were also made for specific events, including coronations, royal weddings and anniversaries. Today, special crackers are made for the royal family.

At the time of writing, 2019, records may have been broken but in December 2001 one of the longest crackers made was 207 feet long and constructed by the parents of children at Ley Hill School and Pre-School, Chesham, Buckinghamshire, UK. When pulled by the children it contained balloons, toys and jokes. A very large cracker was pulled by 1478 people, an event organized by Honda Japan in 2009.

**Why was the snowman rummaging in the
bag of carrots?**

He was picking his nose.

It was Walter Smith, one of the brothers, who introduced hats into crackers early in the 1900s. Crackers are usually pulled before eating dinner, so that everyone gets a flimsy tissue hat, easily torn, and everyone looks equally silly wearing it during the meal. The tradition of wearing hats at Christmas, always a crown, and at other special events, goes back to the Saturnalia celebrations. A mock crown would be given to the chosen king or queen of mirth on the twelfth night. It is also thought by some, to represent the crown worn by the three Wise Men, bearing gifts.

**What did Cinderella say when her photos didn't
arrive on time?**

One day my prints will come.

It was in the 1930s that love messages or poems, were replaced with jokes – very bad jokes. The jokes are usually the question-answer type relying on puns. The writers cleverly use words with different meanings and make up words. It is when one is given the answer to the question, that groans are heard, laughing at oneself, along with others for not seeing the obvious and knowing we have been tricked. Nearly always someone asks, 'Who writes this trash?' Just one more to finish the chapter, a family favourite,

**What is white and crumbly and swings
through the jungle?**

A merangutang.

Greetings

Penned greetings can be traced back to the 1400s. In particular, Valentine's Day greetings in the form of poems. Suitors would sing or recite a romantic verse to their loved one. In 1415 a Valentine's poem was sent by Charles, Duke of Orleans, at that time incarcerated in the Tower of London, to his wife (British Library in London). A Valentine's message was sent in 1477 in letter form, to John Paston from Margery Brews who wrote, 'my right well beloved Valentine'.

But the first Christmas greetings card was produced in 1843.

Sir Henry Cole, the founder of the Victoria and Albert Museum, had a problem, if having numerous friends can be considered a problem. Many people were able to take advantage of the introduction of the Penny post 1840, for cards and letters to be sent anywhere in the country. The volume of post increased dramatically, hence his dilemma. How, he wondered, could he possibly answer so many letters in 1843, sending him seasonal

Circa 1910

37

greetings in a short time? Not to answer was a breach of etiquette.

Having formed an idea, he approached his friend, JC Horsley an artist and member of the Royal Academy, and asked him for a design. This was printed onto as a triptych card, and at the bottom a caption read, 'A Merry Christmas and a Happy New Year to You'. The centre portrayed a family enjoying a Christmas meal together. This scene was flanked by pictures of the poor receiving help from well-wishers. However, the dinner scene was controversial to the Temperance Society, as young children seemed to be enjoying a glass of wine with the family. The card, signed by Cole, was deemed a success by Cole's friends, colleagues and family: Henry sent one to his Grandmother.

Horsley sent one to Cole, and in the bottom right corner added a small self-portrait and 'Xmasse, 1843', instead of his signature. In the following years cards were exchanged and saved much time for the senders. The Temperance Society criticism did not stop Cole going ahead. In 1846, he had a thousand copies printed, selling them at one shilling. These were expensive at the time, and it was thought that Cole's idea would fail.

As we now know, the venture did not fail. The idea caught on, and many in the publishing world by 1887 had copied the idea and developed a flourishing market. Competitions were organized by card publishers, with cash prizes offered for the best designs. Early cards had pictures of flowers, animals and children, to hint at the coming of Spring in the gloomy wintertime. Queen Victoria, not un-like Elizabeth II, sent cards of her family celebrating the festival or of royal events during the year. In 1885, there was much criticism of cards depicting children enjoying the snow and 'angels floating in mid-air bearing a babe'. The *Art Amateur* magazine, 1885, found fault with cherubs whose heads were 'too intangible connected with the body even for a disembodied spirit'. In 1881, A German immigrant to the United States, Louis Prang, who opened a lithographic shop six years earlier, was producing more than a million cards a year.

Joyce Hall began a small postcard printing company in 1905. Later he was joined by his brothers Rollie and William and the company was first known as Norfolk Post Card Company, shortened later to the Norfolk Card Company. In 1913, the company was renamed The Hall Brothers. They realised that on a postcard there was not enough room for senders to write much in the way of greetings. It was in 1925 they introduced the folded Christmas card with twee cliché messages inside and an envelope was added to the purchase. The early cards were mostly of Santas or the star of Bethlehem. Although his brothers were unsure, in 1928 Joyce Hall introduced the now famous Hallmark name. He changed the wording on the back of the cards from 'Hall Brothers Company' to 'A Hallmark Card'. It wasn't until 1954 that the company finally became known as Hallmark Cards.

There were, and are, many card manufacturers, and competition was high to seek originality. Among contributors commissioned to submit designs were Jacqueline Kennedy, Salvador Dalia and Winston Churchill. One card, designed by Ruth Morehead in 1977, called Three little Angels has, to date, proved to be the most popular. Three innocent looking cherubs, two in prayer and the other, one is led to believe might be more mischievous, has her halo a little lop-sided. To date, over thirty-four million copies have been sold. Some popular Victorian cards showed postmen delivering mail, who were called 'robins' because of their red uniforms. One last point to mention, the British Post Office, as it was once known as, used to deliver the post on Christmas morning.

Birds and Beasts

A number of beasts and mini beasts are associated with long held Christmas folklore and it is surprising how many people do not know of them. Those who do know them will, perhaps, enjoy remembering them.

Could it be true that only on Christmas Eve, animals are given a human voice for one hour? A fifth century Christian poet, Aurelius Prudentius Clemens, began this idea, saying that they joined the angels in praising the birth of Jesus. Should you hear them, then you can be sure of very bad luck as they often predicted death. However, to overcome this, the animals are wise enough not to speak if anyone is near. Not in a human voice, but as a crowing cock is thought to drive away evil spirits, he crows throughout Christmas Eve night.

Many people believe that the robin, so prominent on Christmas cards, dates back to Victorian times when the postmen were nicknamed 'robins' because they wore red coloured uniforms. However, robins association with

Christmas goes back much further. Many think that it is lucky to see a robin at Christmas time as some believe it has a drop of God's blood on its chest. To kill one would invite trouble, including turning cow's milk bloody. To steal their eggs from nests was thought to leave the thief with crippled fingers.

A fable tells of the robin's presence in the Bethlehem stable. A fire had been lit and was blazing fiercely but Mary had been distracted. The robin fearing the baby's face might be burned stationed himself between the fire and the child and puffed up its feathers to protect the infant. But, the robin was too close to the fire and its chest was scorched and reddened. This redness stayed with all future generations of robins. In yet another fable, the robin kept a low fire alight by fetching twigs. Again, it is said, he scorched his chest when the flames leapt up. Mary thanked and praised the robin for all it had done. She looked tenderly at its red breast, burned by the flame, and said, 'From now on, let your red breast be a reminder of your thoughtful deed.'

Another story tells of the owl. It was daytime and sleepy owl woke up and was told that Jesus had been born and all the birds and creatures were going to the stable to welcome him. 'I'll come later,' the owl said and went back to sleep. When he woke he was alone, there was no one to tell him where to go. 'Who will take me to the stable?' he kept asking? And now we hear him still asking: 'Who? Who? Who?'

Another bird fable tells of the stork. Baby Jesus was surrounded by an assortment of birds and beasts that had come to greet him, including a stork. It saw the baby lying in the straw with no pillow so it plucked feathers from its plumage to make a soft pillow. From that day on storks are a symbol of birth and feature on cards and presents for new arrivals. It is said if one spots a stork flying in the air or on the roof a house, it is considered a lucky omen as the stork is now referred to as the patron of 'babies'. And when as a child, were we not told that the stork had brought our new brother or sister?

There are two versions about cats – tabbies in particular. The first tells of how the baby was cold and uncomfortable in the makeshift bed. A tom tabby cat heard the child's distressing cries and jumped into the manger and curled itself around the infant to keep him warm. Mary was so grateful to the cat and gently stroked its forehead. Look carefully and you will see the mark of Mary on the head of tabby cats. It is said the letter M would forever be a token of Mary's love.

The second tells how Mary and a tabby both gave birth in the stable. During their labour, Mary bent over the cat sharing her birth pangs. She placed her hand on the cat's head in sympathy saying that they were both new mothers. To this day the mark – M – is prominent on cats' heads. It is unclear how these legends began as there seems to be no mention of cats anywhere in the Bible.

Christmas trees are nearly always festooned with tinsel and it is interesting to know that, in folklore, spiders are responsible for this tradition. Again, there are a number of explanations.

The first tells us that on Christmas Eve, a housewife determined to clean her home from top to bottom, banished spiders to the attic. When the family was asleep, the spiders decided to see what the fuss was about. They were curious about the tree and scrambled all over it from top to bottom. Their activities caused their silk to be woven in and out of the branches. Next morning the family were enchanted to see such fine threads decorating the tree.

A similar story tells of a poor family unable to decorate their tree. The spiders took pity on them and covered the tree overnight with their webs. In the morning, the sun shone on the fine silk threads making them sparkle to the delight of the children.

A third story suggests that when Herod's soldiers were looking for the family, they hid in a cave. They were tired and afraid of being found. A spider overheard their worries and set about weaving its silken thread over the mouth of the cave. When the soldiers came across the cave, they decided that no one could be in the cave as the dense web across the mouth would have been broken. The humble spider had saved the family. Tinsel, it is said, on Christmas trees are replicating spiders' silken threads. Incidentally, the garden spider is identified by the cross on its back.

Ever wondered why moths are attracted to light? A Christmas legend gives an explanation. All the creatures and birds were hurrying to go and see the new baby. The moth was busy cleaning her home and noticed how excited they all seemed and asked where they were going. They told her and said, 'Come with us.'

'I'm too busy right now,' she replied. 'But as soon as I have finished I shall come. How do I find the baby?'

You will see a star giving out a bright light shining over the stable where he is resting.'

When she starting out there was no one to ask the way – she was too late. So now you will see her flying round and round any bright light in the dark trying to find the baby.

Yet another story of the past. If on Christmas Eve, if you hear bees humming, folklore will assure you that they are humming the hundredth psalm that begins, 'Shout for joy to the Lord, all the earth'. And one more of many delightful legends. According to folklore, all animals, at the stroke of midnight on Christmas Eve, kneel in homage to Jesus. Thomas Hardy's poem, 'The Oxen' begins, 'Christmas Eve, and twelve of the clock, Now they are all on their knees.' It is said that cattle knelt beside the manager and gently blew their breath on the baby to keep Him warm.

Such enchanting tales, long may they be told.

What's on Your Christmas Dinner Plate?

Was it turkey, served golden brown, hot and steaming for the head of the house to carve? Perhaps it was sliced earlier, and put ready for consumption on warmed plates? Turkey is a popular choice today. The family coat of arms of William Strickland of Yorkshire, depicts a turkey cock, so it is thought, that after obtaining six birds from American Indians on a voyage around 1526, he brought them to England and sold them. In Saint Andrew's church at Boynton, Yorkshire, there is a lectern carved in the shape of a turkey, with the bible supported on its outstretched tail feathers.

For hundreds of years, what you had for your Christmas dinner, depended entirely on your station in life. Rich folk would most likely have dined on roast goose, woodcock, bustards, peacocks or boar's head. The boar's head was stripped of all flesh, soaked in brine, wrapped firmly in a cloth, then boiled for five or six hours. The pickled boar's meat, including the ears and feet, were pounded into a mince with vinegar, peppers, salt and sage to make up a brawn, and finally stuffed into the cooked boar's head. Those in the Royal favour might have a swan, with the king's permission. Alternatively, there was venison. Cows and chickens were spared the festive table as cows gave milk and chickens laid eggs, essential commodities throughout the year.

The poor, if they were able to afford any meat for the table, would have dined on a goose, purchased from the church, at the cost of a week's wages, around seven pence. Alternatively, they would benefit from the less favoured meat of venison – known as noumbles. The name changed to 'umbles during the fifteenth century and were made up of the heart, liver, ears, tongue and brains. These would be mixed with vegetables to make up 'umble pie. As 'umble pie was eaten by folk of a humble background, this might be the basis of the 'eat humble pie' saying, inferring perhaps one should apologise for a poor word or deed.

Geese, from the first Elizabethan times, would be walked from Norfolk and the Midlands to London, setting out in August, for the Christmas market. In order to protect their feet for this long walk, geese wore leather boots.

To fit these was a difficult task. Later, dipping their feet in tar, then sand, proved far simpler. The geese would be driven through a mixture of soft tar and sand, which would give a very hard-wearing coat when it set. They fed on stubble left in fields after the harvest and there were feeding stations along the route. By the end of the nineteenth century turkey was more readily available to many, although goose was still a popular choice.

At the beginning of the nineteenth century, for better off families, turkey was still the first choice for the festive meal. For lesser-off folk, turkey or chicken was still too expensive, and they made do with a rabbit or goose. Although turkeys were still a favourite, beef proved to be overtaking the Christmas favourite later in the century. Larger joints were now more readily available due to improved farming husbandry – cattle breeding and dairying. Brawn had lost its place, as a broth, containing dried fruits and alcohol, overtook its popularity.

The first and second world wars dramatically altered Christmas fare. The First World War was, in a number of ways, harsher for civilians where food was concerned. Unless they were wealthy, their festive meal would be a cheap cut of beef, stewed and served with Yorkshire puddings. Vegetables were scarce, but people, where possible, grew potatoes and turnips. 'Afters' were a mock plum pudding made from vegetables, sweetened with carrots and, if available, mixed peel and raisins; or perhaps, first served to soldiers, a steamed rice pudding with a dollop of carrot marmalade, and known as Trench Pudding.

The wealthy, if they were lucky, would start their meal with soup, followed by a stuffed goose or turkey or a cut of roast beef and home grown vegetables. Dessert would be a plum pudding, no doubt modified, followed by fruit and nuts.

Rationing in the Second World War was strict. Purchasing many foods required coupons as well. For Christmas, thrifty housewives would save their coupons for months in order to get dried fruit, sugar and other foodstuffs to make their puddings or mincemeat, alongside eggless sponges. For Christmas dinner, if no turkey could be bought, chicken was the next best thing. Some housewives were adept at creating fake Christmas fare, and would fashion a mock turkey out of lamb. For some, it was likely to be roast rabbit with carrots, tin peas, potatoes and cabbage. The rich tried to get the traditional turkey or goose, but often only mutton or beef were available.

Through the ages, Christmas dinners have changed very little. 2016 retail figures reveal that turkey still proves to be popular, not so much a whole one but the leg or breast. If labelled 'ready to cook', less effort is required to prepare the joint, much easier to handle, shorter cooking time and little waste. Roasting chickens proved to be equally popular, and it would seem ducks and geese are making a come-back. You may notice that the pig (pork) was not included in the special dinners down the centuries, except the boar's head. This is because pork, for the most, was easily available through the year. It was common for the less well-off to buy a piglet in spring, and rear it in the garden on or common land. Once it was slaughtered late in the year, it would feed a family throughout winter. Care had to be taken when choosing a piglet – hence the expression, 'don't buy a pig in a poke'. Another saying associated with keeping pigs is, 'a piggy bank'.

Unlike the past when everything was done from scratch, today's Christmas dinner can be purchased already prepared. There are roast potatoes, parsnips, Brussel sprouts, gravy and pigs-in-a-blanket. Also, a very wide, and tempting, variety of desserts.

In the 1800s, pigs-in-a-blanket was an entirely different recipe compared to today. In the recipe that appeared in Maria Parola's cookbook of 1882, oysters were seasoned with salt and pepper, and rolled in a rasher of bacon. This was held together with a toothpick, then grilled or fried until the bacon was cooked. The finished dish would then be served on toast. Sausages, usually pork, have been substituted for the oysters, so at last, pork has a place on the Christmas Day dinner plate.

Vegetables, of course, are a must on your Christmas dinner plate, although many people are happy to go without. Since the nineteenth century it has been a tradition to include – love or hate them – Brussel sprouts. For some, their dinner would not be complete without them. Others tolerate them. But some diners view them with absolute horror, especially children. Added to their misery is the admonishment, 'Eat up. They're good for you.' Indeed, they have many essential vitamins. The flavour of sprouts is, shall we say, distinctive. Much depends on the cooking. Overcooked and they become slimy and smell awful, undercooked and they are al dente. The fact remains, they will appear on your plate and probably cause much controversy.

These mini cabbages were cultivated during the thirteenth century in Ancient Rome. They first appeared in Holland and Belgium (thus the name, Brussels) during the sixteenth century, gradually reaching other European countries. They were widely available in Britain late nineteenth century, so perhaps we must blame the Victorians for their place on the plate. When all is said and done, they are miniature cabbages and perhaps they were a novel idea to add colour to the dish. They are a winter vegetable, with well over a hundred varieties, are easily grown and mature within 180 days. Many believe they are much improved after a frost, right in the middle of the festive season. So it seems, it is a tradition we are stuck with. Finally, would you believe, they are said to improve fertility!

So, just what will be on your plate this year?

Sweet Foods at Christmas

What we eat at Christmas are mostly from hundreds of years old recipes and traditions. These have been modified throughout the ages as foods, once too expensive for the poor, became more readily available and pastoral and civil laws changed. One of the changes is, without doubt, the cake.

Twelfth Night, sixth of January, was celebrated before Henry VIII's reign, particularly amongst the gentry who always invited their servants. These parties included games, drinking and plenty of eating. The centre of the repast was the Cake. Early cakes were more like boiled plum porridge and very slushy, until flour, eggs and butter were added. Included in the ingredients were a dried pea and dried bean. The male who had the bean in his slice of cake was king for the night and the pea designated the queen – so if a servant was elected they ruled or misruled supreme over their masters. (At the end of the Roman Saturn festival, the poor Lord of Misrule was put to death).

In the nineteenth century, these types of party celebrations were still popular, but the bean and pea were omitted. Instead the cake was decorated with frosting, softer and creamer than the royal icing that is more popular today. Usually small Plaster of Paris ornaments topped the cake as well.

There is archaeological evidence that suggests that sugar from cane has been around since 8000 BC, but it was the Crusaders who brought back to Europe the 'honey powder'. In the 1600s, Oliver de Serres discovered how to crystallize sugar in beet.

In the seventeenth century, icing of cakes was a far cry from today's techniques. Sugar and egg white were boiled together then the mixture spread onto the cake. The cake was put back in the oven and when removed after a while, the icing cooled into a hard, glistening covering.

Today's cake also includes a covering of marzipan – a sweet, almond delight with its own history. It is thought to have originated in China and others suggest it came to Europe, courtesy of the Crusaders, from Persia who traded with the East. In Persia it was considered to have medicinal properties.

Marzipan was known by different names across Europe, Spain called it, *postre regio*, in Sicily it was known as *panis martius* or march bread. There is yet another explanation of the name. Small boxes containing spices were known as *mataban* in Germany and the word changed to mean what was in the box – that is marzipan. The French called it *massepain* and is known as *mazapane* in Italy.

Only royalty and the rich could afford this luxury, but once cheap sugar from beet was obtained it became affordable for everyone. So, today's Christmas cake has come a long way from the humble beginnings of the porridge of the past.

In the Middle Ages, pie crusts were no more than flour and water mixed to a dough firm enough to hold meat and the pastry thrown away after eating the contents. Again it is thought the spices the Crusaders brought back changed plain meat fillings, and became the basis for a well-loved Christmas treat – the mince pie. At one time it was called, 'wayfarers' pies' and given to visitors at Christmas time.

Early pies, not too far from modern pies contained raisins, lard, cheese, pork or other meat, wine, figs, expensive spices, honey and again they were only baked for the rich and seen as a status symbol at Christmas.

These pies were served at Christian festivals, but at Christmas the pastry took on the shape of the manager Jesus slept in, and dough babies wrapped in swaddling clothes were placed on top. During the seventeenth century, the 'idolatrous' pastry baby disappeared during the Civil War. In the nineteenth century, meat was excluded from mince pies, although some of today's recipes include suet.

The Stollen Cake originated in Germany probably in the sixteenth century. Early cakes were made from flour, yeast, oil and water. These few ingredients could only be used at Advent. It was then considered a time of fasting and luxury butter and spices were banned. The dough was shaped to represent the baby Christ in swaddling clothes. It was Pope Nikolaus V who gave permission to use butter instead of oil to the family of Prince Ernst of Saxony mid fifteenth century. However, the ban for the general public was not lifted until the end of the seventeenth century. The cake is now baked all over the world and not confined to Christmas. Bakers have their own, as well as the original recipes, but there are only around 150 bakers who are allowed to make the official Dresden Stollen cake endorsed with the seal of the city's famous king – Augustus the

Strong. This name was given to him after his death. It is said many witnessed the prince break an iron horse shoe with his bare hands. Recently, experts have confirmed that horseshoes become brittle with age!

Christmas puddings were once a savoury dish of meat and vegetables. It is thought to have evolved from early mince pie recipes or frumenty, a kind of soup served at the beginning of a meal. Once dried fruit – raisins, currants, prunes – and spices were added, the pudding became known as plum pudding. The Christmas pudding enjoyed today became popular it is believed, when George I declared he had enjoyed his Christmas pottage.

Stir up Sunday conjures up the picture of busy housewives, their families and cooks stirring the contents of the pudding. Every person who stirs the mixture makes a wish. However, Stir up Sunday derives its name from the 1549 Book of Common prayer that is intoned on the last Sunday before Advent – 'Stir up, we beseech thee, O Lord the wills of thy faithful people ...'

It was thought at one time, Christmas recipes included thirteen ingredients to represent Christ and his twelve disciples.

Another tradition dictates that the stirring is done from East to West to depict the three wise men's journey. The sprig of holly that decorates the top of the finished dish is said to represent the crown of thorn. In the Middle Ages it was thought to bring good luck and have healing powers. The brandy, once it is alight, is thought to represent the Passion.

A further tradition was the placing of silver good luck charms in the mixture, later silver coins. This tradition could probably date back to the thirteenth century Twelfth Night Cake. Now, some families, before the pudding is served after dinner, place sterile coins on the plate underneath the serving of pudding.

Mention has already been made of Pagan human sacrifices. This horrific tradition was ended when the church introduced a biscuit shaped in human form to be eaten. There is a tale that possibly has some truth in it, that Elizabeth I asked her cooks to bake the biscuits in the shape of her, readily recognized, courtiers. She suggested that they add chopped ginger mint to enhance the flavour. Thus, gingerbread men were born.

Ever wondered about the striped peppermint candy cane? This is said to represent the shepherd's crook. This would remind the congregation of the shepherds' visit to the stable. One suggestion is that it was given to fretful children or choirboys to keep them quiet during the Christmas mid-night mass, or could it be the letter J to stand for Jesus? Three hundred years ago it was a pure white sugar stick. The white of the cane was to represent the goodness of Christ and the red colouring represented his blood. The hardness of the cane is thought to remind everyone that the church is as solid as rock. These are a few ideas, but I cannot find anything to confirm the true reason. It was early in the twentieth century that the peppermint flavour was added.

Chocolate – a word just as evocative as the word Christmas. The wild cacao trees, found in South America, have been around for over 10,000 years but not cropped until circa 300 BC. The cocoa was introduced to Prince Philip of Spain in 1544, but did not reach the rest of Europe until circa 1650 thanks to an Italian, Antonio Carletti. It was thought that the Spaniards gave it the name of chocolatl. This was a combination of *chocol*, meaning hot a Maya word, and *atl* the Aztec meaning for water. The price of cacao and sugar fell in the early twentieth century and became more affordable.

One tradition linked to Christmas is the chocolate log, whether you buy or make your own, which is much more fun. The log, as you may have guessed, is a link to the winter solstice dating back to the Druid's Solstice celebrations, as discussed in chapter one.

It is a long time to wait for a present on Christmas Day. It was Martin Luther and the German Protestant church who began another tradition – the Advent Calendar. Let the countdown begin! At first twenty-four chalk marks were drawn and one mark each day would be erased. Alternatively, twenty-four straws would be laid in a manager and one removed daily. The first printed Advent Calendar was in 1902 in the form of a clock. The little doors to open each day began in 1920. On opening the door there would be pictures or texts from the Bible. The first chocolate calendar came onto the market in 1958. The daily gift was a chocolate coin, a reminder of the Saint Nicholas gifts for the three unwed girls. Nowadays, there are all sorts of chocolate shapes to be eaten.

Boxes of chocolates as a Christmas present are, of course, always welcome.

Entertainment

For over a hundred and seventy years, in many households the wonderful story by Charles Dickens, *A Christmas Carol*, has been read. It is said that Christmas was re-invented by Charles Dickens. How then, did the story get to be written?

One suggestion is that his father told Charles of his boyhood when he visited Crewe Hall. His grandparents (Charles' great grandparents) were employed there as steward and housekeeper. Elizabeth, the grandmother, was renowned for her storytelling. Some of the tales she told Dickens senior, referred of the magnificent Christmas celebrations at the big house. He in turn, related these stories to his own children.

Another thought is that although Dickens was working on the novel, *Martin Chuzzlewit*, being serialised in a newspaper, it wasn't popular with the readers. Dickens also needed money for his own growing family. So he began writing a Christmas novella, or, as he called it, his 'little Christmas book'.

The 1840s was one of the coldest decades and the country was experiencing an economic crisis. Dickens was disturbed by the growing gap between the wealthy and the increasing numbers of people experiencing poverty. He, because of his own desperate childhood, was committed to social reform. He had witnessed the working conditions of workers in factories and mines, where nine year old children worked over nine hours a day. A visit to a London Ragged School for destitute children shocked him greatly, and when the Government issued a paper outlining the Industrial Revolution's effect on children, he made a public statement about their desperate situations.

Thus, he began his novella and walked at night some fifteen or twenty miles in London, honing his thoughts and plots. As he wrote it is reported that he, 'wept and laughed and wept again'. The story was completed within six weeks, at the end of November 1843, and published on 17 December. This was the turning point in his career. The first printing of six thousand copies was sold out within the week and the book has never been out of print since.

A further idea for the writing of the book suggests that Dickens wanted to encourage the restoration of the seasonal traditions that had been neglected under the Puritans.

Since early childhood, Dickens had been interested in ghosts, the mysteries of the supernatural and magical powers. This curiosity was fostered by the stories told by his nursemaid, Mary Weller. It is not surprising, then, to learn that at least twenty of his books include something of the supernatural. People are often surprised when they talk of four ghosts in the *A Christmas Carol* tale, and are corrected. There is only one ghost, Jacob Marley. The other three, thought to be ghosts, are in fact spirits. It is, of course, the protagonist, Scrooge, who is remembered. A cold, mean-spirited sinner, who wants to avoid Christmas, but his character is changed by the end of the book. We learn he determines to change his ways and becomes more generous and empathic with those who are suffering.

The first dramatisation of *A Christmas Carol* was in London February 1844, three months after its publication, supposedly endorsed by Dickens. To his dismay, he did not receive any remuneration from any of the performances.

It was ten years after publication 1853, that Dickens gave his first, three hour long, performance of the book, in Birmingham. In all his performances he took on the role of each character.

Like a number of performers today who have rituals and talismen to ensure a perfect performance, so did Charles Dickens. It is reported that on the day of performance, he would have two tablespoons of rum flavoured with fresh cream for breakfast, drink a pint of champagne for tea and half an hour before appearing on stage, he would drink a beaten raw egg in sherry. Sometimes, during the interval he might down a cup of beef tea. He always wore full evening dress sporting a buttonhole and a gold watch chain. His last performance was in St James's Hall in London on 15 March 1870 when he made it known that it was his last performance.

Since then, many stage and film productions have acted out the scenes envisaged by Dickens. The earliest incomplete film, a silent film was in 1901. Another silent film was made in 1910 and covered the main issues of the story, and lasted thirteen minutes – thirteen minutes! Another silent film was made in 1923, and critics stated that it 'was very atmospheric'. This was revived in 1935 and became the first talking version of the classic.

In 1938, the first American edited version was produced.

Many interpretations of Ebenezer Scrooge have been portrayed since then. These include a Walt Disney cartoon, *Scrooge McDuck* 1983 and *Mister Magoo's Christmas Carol* 1962. However, it is thought by many, that the 1951 film entitled, *Scrooge* featuring Alastair Sim as Scrooge, was the best version every produced.

Besides *A Christmas Carol* stage plays and films, there are many popular Christmas themed films. Where to start? One of the most popular is, *It's A Wonderful Life*. The story tells how a man's business is ambushed and how desperate he is for his family at Christmas. Not going to spoil the story, but an angel is involved. Another popular film is *Miracle on 34th Street*. The earliest film of this story is 1947 and there have been a number of re-issues. This is a warm-hearted, family film that questions the existence of Santa Claus. Perhaps not so well known, but one of my favourites is, *The Bishop's Wife* and again a Christmas Angel comes to the rescue. Not intended as a Christmas story, nevertheless, *The Snowman* by Raymond Briggs has a firm place since 1982 on national television. The animated characters, James and the Snowman, have some exciting adventures overnight, but come the dawn ...

This chapter is headed entertainment and families have their own well-loved traditional ways of entertainment often including board games. What fun and recriminations there are when granddad or an aunt cheats – even if they didn't, a great deal of teasing and accusations often ensue. Every year there seems to be many new games on the market, but the older games remain the most popular.

Board games go back as far as 5000 BC. A great number of games depend on the fall of the dice. In a burial mound in Turkey, painted stones were found and thought to be the earliest gaming pieces identified. Later, dice found in other burial sites were made of different materials. These included carved bones, turtle shells and wood. Always popular, are the games of Ludo, Snakes and Ladders and Draughts, suitable for young and old alike. Monopoly demands much more from the player, and perhaps gives an insight to our would-be ruthless business-minded relatives!

Playing cards lend themselves to all sorts of fun from snap for the youngest to more demanding skills from adults. Cards, too, have an interesting history. The earliest mention of playing cards, known as the 'leaf game' was played in China, circa 860. Paper cards were produced around 1005. There is evidence that card games had reached Europe by the thirteen hundreds. A Swiss document decreed that their use was banned in Bern at that time.

At first, the card suits included hearts, bells, leaves acorns and swords. The familiar suits of today, hearts, spades, clubs and diamonds, were first produced by the French in the fifteen hundreds. The 1790's French revolution demoted the King as top card, giving place to the Ace.

Another tradition after lunch for some, when everyone has over-eaten, is to listen to the broadcast of the Queen's Speech at 3.00 p.m. In 1932 this was considered the best time so that countries in the British Empire would receive it by short wave signals. The first royal Christmas message, live on the radio from Sandringham, was made by King George V, the Queen's grandfather. The speech was the suggestion of the Prime Minister, Ramsey MacDonald and written by Rudyard Kipling. The two and half minute speech was two-hundred and fifty-one words long and heard by over twenty million people. To disguise the rustling of papers and the suggestion that the king was trembling, the table was covered with a thick cloth.

It was in December 1937, that George VI made his first Christmas broadcast. This was no easy task for a shy man who had to overcome a severe speech impediment to fulfil the now established tradition of speaking to his subjects. Queen Elizabeth II's first Christmas broadcast was in 1952 and her first Christmas televised speech was in 1959. Her Majesty writes her own message, within a religious structure, telling of her family and current events.

Yet another form of Christmas entertainment is a visit to a pantomime. No matter if it be a lavish professional production or a local amateur group who give their very best, the shows are always lively and colourful. They are sometimes silly and always noisy. Nearly always the panto is based on a traditional children's story – Aladdin, Cinderella, Jack and the Beanstalk or Peter Pan to name a few. Perhaps, something the audience enjoys most is, what is termed, audience participation. This means always cheering the Dame, who is usually a well padded male, and booing the baddie. And who can resist shouting out a warning to the hero/heroine, 'He's behind you', when the baddie appears or arguing with another performer who extols their non-existent virtues.

Baddie: I'm the best son in the world!
Audience: Oh, no you're not!
This is repeated, as tradition demands, only three times.

Always the show ends with an audience sing-a-long.

The word pantomime is made up of panto, Greek for 'all' and the Latin word 'mime' meaning 'imitator' or 'actor'. Mime nowadays usually refers to a drama or play without words. The actual word pantomime was coined in the eighteenth century. Some think that pantomime performances are based on the Lord of Misrule of earlier times, but is believed by others to have had its beginnings in Italy during the sixteenth century. The Commedia dell'arte, was a street theatre and included comedy, tumbling, acrobatics and long-standing favourite characters. These included and old man, Pantalone, a clown Pierrot and Columbine who loved the servant, Arlecchino, or Mr Punch as he is known in the UK. These characters formed part of comic plays from the late 1600s and were introduced by John Rich, into London circa 1730. Rich was an actor-manager of the Lincoln's Inn Theatre and The Theatre Royal, in Covent Garden.

Over the centuries, plots, costumes and up-to-date topics have been added or altered and it is to the Victorians that a Christmas visit to the pantomime was established. One thing is for sure, young and old and those in between, can be seen leaving the theatre with a broad smile on their faces.

There is no doubt about it! The school nativity play is eagerly awaited by excited children and proud parents every year. Teachers might be a little less enthusiastic! The planning begins immediately after the mid-Autumn half-term holiday. The younger the child, the more daunting the challenge. Who shall be Mary, Joseph, the innkeeper, the angel, star, donkey, shepherds? A part must be found for every child. The children need to become familiar with the nativity story, but Christmas is seven or eight weeks ahead. Depending on the age of the child, a suitable script must be written. Then there are the costumes. Is there anything in the dressing up box? Or can we ask parents to come up with something suitable? As a mother, for one son I dressed him in a red velvet curtain and made a crown to fit him out as a king. For the other lad, the striped tea cloth served as a headdress when he was given the part of a shepherd.

And then the teacher allocates the parts – children and sometimes over-zealous parents battle for the most important roles. *Mumsnet,* one year, revealed that one mother was bragging that her child had the head part, he definitely had; he was the head end of the donkey.

At the end of the term – the grand performance! Very few go as planned. There is always the child who seems fixed to the floor and has to be moved manually by the teacher. Others fidget, pick their noses, nudge others and, touchingly, wave or call out to their family in the audience. On the Internet there are many such mishaps. Some of my favourites from dayurseries.co.uk include:

'As Mary and Joseph took up their positions, one of the preschool staff sidled up to the narrator and passed her a teddy wrapped in a blanket. 'What's this?' she hissed. 'We've forgotten the baby, Jesus, this will have to do!'

Where was Wise Man 3? We waited with baited breath, we looked to the wings. Suddenly, Wise Man 3 darted out to the centre of the stage and shouted 'Mum, it's my bit, are you watching?!'

'When Mary was naming the Baby Jesus, she lifted him up and said in the biggest, clearest voice, very proudly, "I think I'll call him Colin"!'

And *Mumsnet* shared the following:

'A fight broke out over who was going to hold baby Jesus so Joseph pushed Mary off the stage.'

Yes, indeed it is a stressful time for teachers, but my colleagues and myself wouldn't want to ever change such a magical, rewarding time.

Francis of Assisi began the presentation of the Nativity in 1223 to bring the story to the congregation unable to understand the message being intoned in Latin. After seeking permission from the Pope, Francis set up the first nativity in the Italian town of Greccio. From a friend he borrowed some animals and straw to represent the stable. There was a live donkey and oxen, and local shepherds kept watch over their flocks in nearby fields. The infant Jesus was made of wax, and the roles of Mary and Joseph were in costumes. The tableau was as near as possible to the first Christmas, so that the people might share the experience. Through the centuries, angels, camels and three kings have been added.

According to Saint Bonaventure, people saved the hay from such performances as it was thought that cattle which ate the hay afterwards would be cured of disease.

If you haven't already, a visit to a performance of *The Nutcracker* ballet, will be a very rewarding treat. The story of *The Nutcracker and the Mouse King* by Hoffmann, set to music by Tchaikovsky, and exquisitely danced, is a delight. The first performance was in 1892 in St Petersburg and met with much criticism. One complained that it was a ballet produced for children and performed by children. Others considered it insipid and tedious and that in Act Two the dancers looked like food in pastry shop. However, A Russian newspaper wrote, 'It is hard to say which number is the greatest, for everything from start to finish is beautiful.' And another wrote: that 'Tchaikovsky's orchestral writing was the work of genius'. It was 1934 before the ballet reached London theatres.

In German folklore, it was thought that nutcrackers were given as Christmas presents to families to protect the home and banish evil spirits. The early designs were usually of animals or birds, but in the seventeenth century they were carved into kings and soldiers. The ballet is set on the magical Eve of Christmas. There is the tree (and what a tree!), masses of presents and family and friends – a story suitable for all ages.

🎄 🎄 🎄

Well, here we are at the end of our look at Christmas facts, fiction and feasts. Do not think that what you have read in this tiny tome is complete. There is more, so much more! As each custom was unwrapped like a Christmas gift, I was fascinated by the history inside every one.

I set out to make this a light-hearted and not over serious read, so have tried not to saturate the reader with too many facts and figures but the historical background is a truly engaging explanation of our Christmas festivities.

Nor have I lost sight of the fact that this is, first and foremost, an important Christian festival. The very word Christmas is the combined words of *Mas* and the name of Christ from the Greek word Χριστός (Khrīstos), meaning the chosen one. The first letter X is sometimes used as a shortened word for Christmas, Xmas. The Greeks translated the word from the Hebrew word Māšîa and it was later translated into English to mean 'Messiah'. The suffix 'mas' comes from an old English word, maesse, meaning a feast or festival day. There are, of course, other explanations, but this one appealed to me.

I do hope you found the content of interest and that you found it surprising, amusing and curious. But no matter what your own beliefs and religions are, there is no doubt, that Christmas is a time to celebrate, be it a birthday celebration or the welcome return of longer days and the promise of a new year. I wish you all joy and peace.

Acknowledgements

Anne and John Samson – TSL Publications
Ray Holloway – for feeding me ideas to pursue

Internet

A Magazine of Understanding
Ace Collins, Stories Behind the Great Traditions of Christmas
Alison Barnes, History Today, Vol 56, Issue 12, Dec 2006
Ben Johnson – Who were the Druids?
Branfionn NicGrioghair
C Michael Hawn, History of Hymns
Robert J Myers, Celebrations The Complete Book of American Holidays
Charlotte Mackaness
Chrisa Rooks
Coe, Sophie and Michael
Daily Mail
Danny Lewis (Smithsonian.com)
David J Meyer
Ellen Castelow
Elvis Galbreath
Good News
Historic UK

Jack Wellman
The Christian Science Monitor
Jan Whitton
Karen Swallow Prior
Kat Moon
Lawrence Evans, Christmas Tree World
Lucas Reilly
Mashed Radish (Internet)
Maureen Monahan
Penny Travers, ABC Radio talk ,2016
Ronald Hutton, Blood and Mistletoe
Ruth Binney
Sam McRoberts
Sarah Gillespie, Irish Times, April 2019
Songfacts Internet
Stephanie Pappas
The Daily Telegraph
Thesaurus.com
Tom Moore
Vox Internet
Whitney Hopler

Books by Beatrice

Children
The Adventures of Rhys:
Training a Greyhound
Urgent! Pocket Money Required
Disasters and Delights of Family Celebrations
The Sometimes Society
Enormous Responsibilities
When Rhys Fell out a Tree

Towpath Tale series
Towing Path Tales
More Towing Path Tales
A Particular Year

Adult
The Man from the North East
Elusive Destiny
Archie's Children

Plays by Beatrice

A Certain Monday
Connie's Lovely Boy
From Commoner to Coronet
Governed by Magpies
In Less than Ten Minutes
Plays for Young Actors

Please visit Beatrice's web site
http://bholloway.newauthors.eu/
Link to her Facebook page:
https://www.facebook.com/beatrice.holloway.5
Publisher page:
https://tslbooks.uk/authors/beatrice-holloway

www.ingramcontent.com/pod-product-compliance
Lightning Source LLC
La Vergne TN
LVHW021546080426
835509LV00019B/2861